PECULIAR CONFLICTS

AFRICAN MARRIAGES IN WESTERN CULTURES

William Femi Awodele

Copyright © 2003 by William Femi Awodele

Peculiar Conflicts
by William Femi Awodele

Printed in the United States of America

Library of Congress Control Number: 2003100512
ISBN 1-591604-48-6

All rights reserved. No part of this publication may be reproduced or transmitted in any form or by any means without written permission of the publisher.

Unless otherwise indicated, Bible quotations are taken from The New International Version. Copyright © 1995 by Zondervan and Dake's Annotated Reference Bible, King James Version. Copyright © 1997 by Dakes Bible Sales, Inc.

Xulon Press
10640 Main Street
Suite 204
Fairfax, VA 22030
(703) 934-4411
XulonPress.com

To order additional copies, call 1-866-909-BOOK (2665).

DEDICATED

to God Almighty for His grace and favor

and to the boys,

Ibukunoluwa and Fiyinfoluwa

ACKNOWLEDGMENTS

I want to thank our parents for doing a good job raising my wife and myself and giving us a good legacy to pass on to our children – a legacy of strong culture and moral upbringing and, most importantly, a legacy to be Christ-like and heaven-bound.

> Olufadejinmi Sr. and Olalonpe Awodele
> Oluwole and Babafunmike Songonuga

To our siblings for their support, Nimi and Seun Dokubo, Olu Jr. and Sola Awodele, Tunde and Bola Dosu, Femi and Funmi Akinfe, Uche and Bukola Ajoku,

Bankole and Natasha Songonuga, Sola and Yemisi Olaitan, Bunmi Songonuga, Muyiwa Awodele and Tope Songonuga – thank you.

To the Board of Directors and Coordinators worldwide of Christian Couples Fellowship International, Inc., for their belief in the vision that God gave to us, and their strong commitment to reducing the incidence of divorce through the monthly meetings.

To Bola Dosu, Solape Dada, and Kerri DeVries, who went over the manuscript, and Deanne Hedglen for the final editing.

Finally, to the Lord God Almighty, who has made this possible.

W. Femi Awodele

The names of the people involved with the true-life stories in this book were deliberately omitted. Other stories and names in this book were made up by the author, but they reflect the realities that African marriages face in Western cultures.

William Femi Awodele

TABLE OF CONTENTS

Chapter One	African Culture	23
Chapter Two	Western Culture	31
Chapter Three	Clash of Cultures	39
Chapter Four	Peculiar Conflicts	49
Chapter Five	Conflict Resolution – African, Western, or Biblical?	59
Chapter Six	Enjoying Canaan	95

FOREWORD

Many of us have spent a considerable amount of time preparing for our professions or vocations. After qualification or graduation, we have to keep updating our knowledge in a lifelong process in order to stay current. In contrast, it is possible to get married and become parents with very little preparation or instruction. After the wedding, most of us soon realize that we need help. This book has been written to help marriages succeed.

While anyone of any racial background can learn

from the Biblical principles illustrated in this book, the book is particularly germane to those of us who grew up in Africa and have relocated to the Western world.

The author, William Femi Awodele, has been burdened for marriages since he and his wife had significant difficulties in the early years of their marriage. God has now called him out of the corporate world and into full-time ministry to teach the application of scriptural principles to the day-to-day problems people face in their marriages.

We would do well to remember that marriage is an institution that antedates the church and that strong marriages and godly offspring are in the grand design for the propagation of the gospel of our Lord Jesus Christ. Thus the relationship between a man and his wife is compared in the Bible to that between the Lord Jesus and the church.

This book focuses on conflict resolution and the unrealistic expectations we bring into our marriages.

Foreword

Those of us of African descent can immediately relate to the examples given (the examples have come through the author's personal experience and from counseling both in the United States and in England). Conflicts will come in every marriage and the way we resolve these conflicts will determine how strong our marriages will be.

I highly recommend the book to all Christians, especially African Christians. May God use the book as an instrument to bless and enrich our marriages, as we wait for the coming of our Lord Jesus Christ.

M. Olubunmi Dada, M.D, Ph.D.
Family Physician, Professor of Anatomy and Bible Teacher

INTRODUCTION

Kunle and Lonpe married in Nigeria in 1992. Kunle was a mid-level manager in a bank with a promising future. Lonpe was a nurse with a big hospital. He was the main breadwinner in Nigeria; he earned more and therefore he took up most of the household financial responsibilities. Lonpe supported her husband by taking care of small bills, mainly school allowance for the kids (Ayo, 8; Nike, 6; and Tolu, 3) and foodstuff for the house. They did not have a joint account.

They earned enough to get two house-helps, one to

do house chores and the other to take care of the kids while they both went about their long hours at work. Kunle had a company car with a driver.

The couple lived in Lagos, Nigeria, and had family members on both sides around to help out with kids when necessary; grandmas, aunts, uncles, etc., when available. Whenever they had marital conflicts, Lonpe was quick to call one of Kunle's parents who then would call him and would always tell him to treat his wife with respect without asking for the reason of conflict. Kunle also called Lonpe's parents during conflict and their response was always, "Apologize to your husband." They went to church but rarely involved the pastor in their marital problems for fear of exposing the conflicts in their marriage and risking the dignity accorded them by the church.

The lifestyle they lived in Nigeria was such that Kunle was never really home for the kids except on Sundays (to go to church), he had no romantic dates with his wife except for occasional Saturday night parties, he had no part in how the house was taken care of, and he never visited the kitchen to make meals either for himself or his family. Lonpe had no problem with this lifestyle because they had two house-helps, tons of family members around and Kunle provided for most of the family's financial needs.

In 1997, they won the visa lottery and decided to move to America.

Dan was a Kenyan; he lived in Nairobi until age 23 and then went to England to continue his education. He started school in London, working as a security officer during this time as well, and soon completed a bachelor's degree in Business Administration. Upon graduation, Dan joined the department of housing.

After 10 years of Dan being single in London, his parents were concerned about his marital status. They contacted a family about an arranged wedding for their son.

Nana was brought up in Nairobi, Kenya; she went to the local college there and graduated as an attorney.

Dan came to Nairobi on vacation and liked Nana. They did both the traditional and church wedding. Nana moved in with Dan's parents while he went back to England to file immigration papers for her to join him.

During Dan's bachelor years in England he had dated several girls and was used to the way of life in the busy city of London. Nana, on the other hand, had dated only one person in college (no physical relationship), had the values of an extended family unit, and saw her husband as lord and master – especially because of his financial clout and her imagination of what life in London, England, was going to be like.

Nana joined Dan in London in 1999. She soon became disillusioned with Dan (he was doing two jobs) and the lifestyle in London. The young marriage was suffering from unrealistic expectations.

Introduction

Donne and Adzo were Togolese students at the University of Toronto in Canada. They met at the International Students Christian Fellowship on campus. They knew each other for a while but started to date in their final year of school.

Upon graduation they both naturalized and became Canadians. They both were employed and decided to marry. At the time of their marriage Donne had lived in Canada for 8 years and Adzo for 5 years.

After marriage, Donne wanted his wife to be a typical African wife (what he had seen his Mom do). Adzo, however, would not have any of that "nonsense" because she felt that although they were Africans, they had lived in Canada for a long time and no such "slavery" would happen.

The above are everyday stories of immigrants moving from Africa to European countries and North America. This book is about what awaits them in London, Berlin, Paris, New York City, Chicago, etc., in terms of cultural differences and how they can survive the conflicts without breaking up their marriages.

It is hoped that after reading this book the incidence of divorce among African immigrants will be greatly reduced. I pray that this book will provide a starting point for couples to talk about the issues they face in their own situation and how to resolve them using their cultural backgrounds as assets in their new environment.

Femi Awodele

CHAPTER ONE

African Culture

Africa is the second-largest continent and is second in population. Civilization is said to have started in the horn of Africa and the Bible records the early Egyptian civilization during the days of the Pharaohs.

Africa is currently a 52-state continent (with several Islands) and it is divided into five major sub-divisions for political reasons – West Africa, North Africa, East Africa, Central Africa and South Africa. While the people and geography of Africa are diverse, there is some commonality in its religion and culture.

The African form of religion is generally referred to as animistic (thinking all things in spiritual terms) and polytheistic (recognizing a Supreme God, but believing that you can only approach this God through other gods and not directly). These beliefs encourage the worship of smaller gods such as the god of iron, god of water, goddess of fertility, etc., and deities such as dead family members who are now worshipped. This form of worship involves human and animal sacrifices. There are major emphases on spiritual forces in African religion. Most of these religious and cultural ceremonies were exported to Brazil, Cuba and America during the slave-trade era.

Before Christianity or Islam, kings were the central figures in the African form of government. Kings still are the custodians of the culture and religion, presiding over ceremonies and rituals. Although the kingdoms are monarchical in structure, they are usually democratic in governance. Kings have councils to advise them on matters relating to justice and its dispensation, spiritual issues, and warfare with neighbors or other kingdoms. The king mother is usually a sacred position in this system of government – she has great influence over the king and is very much revered. Major kingdoms are the Zulu empire in South Africa, the Benin Kingdom in West Africa, and the Oyo Kingdom in present-day Nigeria and West Africa.

Christianity came to Africa in the days of the apostles. The Bible mentioned the Ethiopian eunuch who became a Christian and was baptized (*Acts 8:25-39*). The gospel of Christ was spread far and wide within the continent. About 600 years later (in the seventh century), Islam was brought to Africa by followers of the Prophet Mohammed after his death. Some of his followers took the jihad to Africa and conquered many northern African kingdoms. Christian missionaries later returned with Christianity in the late 1800s.

Traditional African marriages are greatly influenced by religion. An African marriage is a socially and legally sanctioned union of two people and their families.

Marriage is seen as the union of two families in most African cultures. The woman at the center of the union is therefore usually treated as property being exchanged in this union.

Men and women usually go through various tests and ceremonies to be declared adults in their communities; these tests differ from one culture to another all over Africa. In some cultures women are usually taken into a fattening house to get them ready for their husbands (the Calabar tribe in Southeastern Nigeria). The practice of polygamy (marriage of more than one woman to a man) is widely accepted, because women are seen as property – the more you have, the better your status. In many African cultures, when a man dies his wife is usually married to a surviving brother.

Marriage is seen as strictly a means of procreation for women (men have concubines and it does not seem to make any difference). Any woman who cannot have children is labeled in the society and sometimes is cast out and made fun of. Not having a male child is also seen as the woman's fault and such women are ostracized. The woman in the wedding is literally being sold, and this explains the high dowry price in some African cultures (among the Ibo in Eastern Nigeria, the dowry depends on the girl's education and parents' status). A dowry is wedding gifts brought by the groom's family to the bride's family – the bride's family usually gives a list to the groom's family ahead of the wedding day.

African societies have undergone social changes as a result of exposure to Christianity, Islam, and colonialism. The introduction of Western education and white-collar jobs completely changed things. Apart from the adoption of Christian and Islamic names, Western education became a very important tool to enhance social status, hence everyone wanted his or her children to be educated before getting married.

A university/college education is very important in many African countries south of the Equator because of the Christian religion. The northern countries with Islamic influences do not really see Western education as important, hence early and arranged marriages are still commonplace.

In high school, the terms boyfriend or girlfriend are common "lingo" in Africa. At this stage there is nothing serious, just two kids who are very fond of each other. There is handholding and some kissing (usually no sexual relationship), but their parents are usually not interested in such relationships. Upon getting to college/university it clearly becomes dating, because both individuals see the relationship as a potential marriage union. Parents also become interested at this point and would welcome any young man or woman brought home by their daughter or son. Typically, if a boyfriend or girlfriend avoids meeting the parents at this point then you can tell he or she is not serious.

Most African couples now meet in college/university. The second-most common place to meet is high school, then work or other places such as fellowship/church, etc. Arranged meetings are still common, with boy and girl requesting it. Dating and courting is not defined in Africa, yet both parties have marriage at the back of their minds when approaching each other. There is no formal ceremony or giving of an engagement ring until the wedding ceremony.

Once the immediate family agrees to the union, both sets of parents send emissaries to look into the other family's background for various illnesses or religious practices. This has broken up many potential couples, but it's a culture that is gradually fading. If the background check comes back positive, then the wedding proceeds. If it's negative, the family advises their son or daughter to look for another person. In spite of the Western influence on modern dating in Africa, individuals still make their choice of partners with the parents' and extended family's preference very much at the back of their minds (things like ethnic background, religion, social status, etc.).

After wedding ceremonies – which may include civil unions, customary or church unions, and even common-law unions – the bride moves into the extended family's house and is expected to respect the other women in the household. If the couple lives in a city, they move into a rented apartment and start their married life.

CHAPTER TWO

Western Culture

Western civilization has its roots in Europe, in the cities bordering the Mediterranean Sea, where separation of urban dweller from nature was considered a desirable outcome of civilization.

Western culture today is an amalgam of cultures (largely, but not exclusively, European) that has undergone – and is undergoing – rapid change. This accelerated change is the product of the industrial and technological revolutions. Unlike most of the cultures that it has absorbed, which had evolved over millennia of relative stability, Western culture is now a culture in transition. (David Klein)

The Western culture as we know it today is a direct result of technological advancement, the influence of European monarchies and the Judeo-Christian values adopted by royal families. The early settlers in America from Europe (the pilgrims) were influenced by these Judeo-Christian values and they incorporated these beliefs into their constitution after fighting with England to gain their independence.

These values formed the basis of what was to become the American culture, where the man went to work and the woman stayed home to take care of the children. Early marriage for women was commonplace; as late as the 1950s people were marrying right out of high school in their late teen years. I have an older American friend who has been married for about 42 years, and her marriage has survived tough times. While waiting in a church hall, she came up to me (she knew I was in marriage ministry) and told me how she had married at 17, how things had been tough and how divorce was not even mentioned during the tough times.

To correct what many believed to be the ills of the culture that prevailed, which was basically the supremacy of the white male, there were revolutions led by women and blacks in America for the right to vote and the right to achieve equality as stated in the U.S. Constitution.

The Cultural Revolution in America (and, subsequently, many European countries) in the late 1950s and 1960s changed a lot of the cultural beliefs. Many of the changes sought to completely erase the prevailing Judeo-Christian values, which were exploited for personal gains before the Cultural Revolution era. According to the Gallup Organization, 21 percent of America thought premarital sex was acceptable in 1969; in 2001, 60 percent thought it was acceptable.

The proponents of these changes knew the best way to effect change was to seek political power, which was achieved at various governmental levels. These governments (local, state and national) have enacted laws that are anti-marriage, promote single parenthood and currently seek to change the definition of marriage to a union of two people who are not necessarily a man and a woman. These anti-Judeo-Christian values of marriage have not only permeated America, but are getting major support in European countries. Today, many Christian organizations fight various laws that seek to eliminate the family as we know it, and many (such as Christian Couples Fellowship International, Inc.) seek to teach the Biblical truth about marriage relationships.

A typical Western family in the present day is a husband and wife with two children (and maybe a dog), probably married late because of their careers. They typically live in a three-bedroom house, with household chores divided between husband and wife (and sometimes the kids). They do not have any house-helps and cannot afford "Merry Maids," but they might occasionally call someone to clean their carpets. Both are usually tired by the time they get back home, regardless of if they live in large cities like New York City, London, or Chicago, or smaller cities such as Omaha, Neb., Aberdeen, Scotland, or Londonderry, Ireland.

The couple and their children oftentimes live far away from extended family members. Grandparents visit occasionally on holidays, or they sometimes visit the grandparents' homes. Because of this geographical separation, the couple is dependent on babysitters or friends when they go on a date. Their dates are usually timed, as both are worried about the kids. They may try to get away alone every three months or so, but that becomes boring because they rent a room only for both of them to sleep throughout the weekend. When they're not sleeping, they're thinking about their kids.

The typical couple's finances are in a mess – they have a lot of debt because they are trying to be like the Joneses, and they are three paychecks away from bankruptcy. They look forward to summer vacation with the kids but dread its expense, and Christmas is a trying time because the kids must get something impressive from Santa (they are Santa – but don't tell the kids). The husband wants a 4-wheel-drive vehicle and the wife wants a minivan because of the kids' soccer and ballet.

The stress of work, running the kids around, and not having time for each other creeps into the marriage and makes it miserable. They sometimes see a marriage counselor, but each usually has a set mind that the fault is the other person's. Once things become unbearable or they "fall out of love" with each other, divorce is always an option (more than 50 percent of American marriages end up in divorce). Television programs and society at large encourage them to get rid of this other person and stay single. Why marry when you can live together without commitment?

CHAPTER THREE

Clash of Cultures

Marital conflict is a disease that affects people from every part of the world, whether in Africa, Asia, Europe or America. Wherever two human beings (with their sinful natures) come together, there is marital conflict. It exists beyond geographical, cultural or economic barriers.

Each society, however, has unique marital conflicts based on its historical background, prevalent culture, economy and standard of living, and spiritual beliefs.

The standard of living of Western countries is

attracting African natives in the thousands to Western Europe and North America. These immigrants face a set of new marital conflicts as they settle in their new countries and homes.

Here are a couple true but entertaining stories of culture shock:

– Having being brought up in Nigeria (a former British colony), I call pants "trousers" and underwear "pants". During my first week in America, I went to work and a colleague complemented my new trousers with, "Femi, I like your pants." I was very embarrassed and looked to see if my trouser zipper was down. It was only later that another Nigerian told me "pants" means trousers in America.

– A friend told me of his own ordeal. Back in the village in Africa, a man can go around the village in a "wrapper" (a gown tied around the waist) with no shirt on. In this friend's first week in Texas, he went out to pick up the newspaper from the driveway, tying a towel around his waist, and with no shirt on. He told me it was the most embarrassing day of his life, as neighbors thought he was crazy (and mentioned what he did to his host later that day).

Historical and Religious Differences

Western culture originated in Europe and was influenced by the industrial and technological revolutions. It also was influenced by Judeo-Christian values, which shaped the prevalent culture from the days of Roman Emperor Constantine to the dissident pilgrims who moved from Europe to settle in America. The culture that emerged recognized men as superior. Men went to work and provided for their families while the women stayed home and took care of the children. Christianity was the religion of choice, either as a conservative or Protestants such as John Wesley and Martin Luther.

Africa has documented existence of humans before Europe. These early settlers were hunters and nomads; as they existed between the ages (Stone Age, Iron Age, etc.), they started to settle down into kingdoms with their own structure of government (monarchical), culture and religion. The prevalent religions of animism and polytheism have greatly influenced the culture to this day (for example, the practice of polygamy).

Cultural Differences

A typical African marriage is a union of two families. The families stay involved from planning the wedding until the couple is old and even after the death of one of them. Family members are sent to live with the couple as soon as they get married to help them. In Western culture, the wedding is strictly a union between the bride and the groom. Afterward, the extended family is expected to give them space.

Elders drawn from both the husband's and wife's families typically resolve conflicts in Africa, while couples in Western countries usually avoid family interference in their problems (although they might seek opinions). Monogamy has been the accepted practice of a Judeo-Christian Western culture, while the African culture has managed to preserve a polygamous culture. Young adults in Western cultures are typically not influenced by parental preference when choosing whom to date (and the test of manhood is getting a driver's license). In African culture, however, serious consideration is still given to parental preference (as evidenced by the ongoing practice of family background checks in parts of Africa).

The two cultures see the roles of man and woman slightly different. Men lead the home in both cultures but wives are more or less property in African culture.

They are expected to work and raise kids at the same time. Western culture recognizes a woman as an equal partner in marriage; most courts award 50 percent of the family value to the woman in the case of a divorce where the woman has been a homemaker. A higher income by the wife would more adversely affect an African man than a Western man.

Economic Differences

The standard of living in both cultures also affects the marital relationship. Couples in Africa don't send flowers nor do they go on hotel getaways because that money would be more useful to feeding the large family (the culture encourages a large family). Romance to many Africans is sex. Many of us Africans never saw affection being shared between our parents or grandparents in the same way it is displayed in Western culture. An average guy in Europe or America probably has seen his Dad take his Mom out to lunch, kiss her, and buy her flowers while very few of us from Africa saw that behavior.

I believe African guys could be romantic and would nourish their spouse if the funds were available, but because the family income is barely enough to provide three meals a day spending money on getaways or flowers becomes a luxury. I know many reading this would say, "You don't have to have money to be romantic." While I agree, having money sure does help. The best romantic thing Ola and I do regularly is to spend the night at a local hotel. The thought of waking up without kids asking for milk or waking up in a different bed with my wife tickles me silly. Yet hotels (in Africa, America, and Europe) charge money, not cowry beads.

Spiritual Differences

As mentioned earlier, African religion before Christianity and Islam was animism and polytheism. Africans see spiritual undertones in every situation of life. They believe that there is a Supreme Being but he is to be worshipped through other, lesser gods. These beliefs were brought into Christianity and Islam as people converted. There are many African churches that allow animal sacrifice and polygamy. Many Islamic sects allow the same.

The downside of these beliefs is that conflicts are not usually dealt with; they get sidetracked with spiritual sacrifices. The Zulu tribe in Southern Africa usually will have two people who are fighting sit opposite each other with a mediator. The mediator summarizes the complaints and asks if both parties are willing to reconcile. If they both agree, each will drink water mixed with ash and spit it out over his own left shoulder. Then they drink beer from the same calabash (gourd cup). The symbolic cooling effect of water points to a spiritual disposition of reconciliation.

Many in Western countries profess Christianity and

the constitutions of such countries reflect Judeo-Christian values. For instance, polygamy is *not* allowed and the practice of it is prosecuted in court. Circumstances are seen as coincidental rather than spiritual. While many Westerners love themselves and love money, they do not see such practices as spiritual. An African in America, however, would see the love of self beyond others as spiritual.

CHAPTER FOUR

Peculiar Conflicts

As Africans move to Europe and America for education and a better standard of living, they bring with them age-old African beliefs, religion, culture, spiritual beliefs, morals, and values. They attempt to mix their ideology with what predominates in their new country of abode.

Most Africans travel to Western cultures with a fantasy-like attitude, thinking that once they get to London or America all their problems will be solved. Instead, they are now faced with a new set of problems that can be devastating if the foundation of their marriage is not strong.

First Scenario

Let's take Kunle and Lonpe as examples. To recap: Both of them were successful in Nigeria with their careers. Kunle, as a banker, earned more and provided for his family without contributing to the household chores. Lonpe could care less about him not helping around the house because they had house-helps. Lonpe also did whatever she wanted with her own income, except for food and the kids' allowances.

After winning the visa lottery and immigrating to America, Kunle could not find a job in the banking industry right away. His friends advised him to take a job driving a taxicab until he could get a bank job. Lonpe, on the other hand, passed her certification exam and got a job as a nurse. These new dynamics now are causing the following conflicts:

1. Kunle's self-esteem is battered; once a manager in an office, now he's a cab driver. He had always earned more than his wife and now he can't deal with her earning more than him.

2. Kunle has never helped around the house with chores or even the kids. Now that they don't have their house-helps, Lonpe is nagging him to bathe the kids, take them to school, make meals sometimes, etc.

3. Their income level is also causing problems. Bills are coming in, they are living from month to month with a lot of stress, and at the same time extended family members are calling from Nigeria for the couple to send money.

Kunle and Lonpe are used to resolving conflicts by going to each other's parents. Unfortunately there are no parents around now and, being new in the community, they are apprehensive about going to the pastor of their new church. They have never been to a marriage therapist, so it did not cross their minds to seek such help.

They eventually discussed their marital conflict with the pastor of a Nigerian-based church, who recommended prayer and fasting to fight against the enemy attacking their marriage but did not deal with the details of their conflicts.

Second Scenario

Nana arrived in London with great expectations of the city and how pleasant life would be. She had these expectations because whenever Dan came home to Nairobi, Kenya, to visit, he would always bring nice things such as fine clothing, jewelry and lots of cash. He also would dress very well, giving Nana the (unspoken) impression that she would be living a fairy-tale lifestyle.

Nana's first surprise was Dan's apartment. She had expected something bigger. Upon arriving in London, Dan bought Nana a train/bus pass so she could get around on her own. The reality that would cause the main conflict, however, was Dan holding down two jobs so he could send money back home to maintain the image of affluence that families in Nairobi had of him (and Nana also had of him). Dan also wanted his wife to dress in the sexy outfits that the European girls wore – tight jeans and revealing shirts – to fulfill his selfish lust.

Nana's way of dealing with the problems was to get close to some non-Christian Kenyans who gave the ungodly advice that Nana should abandon her marriage because of the lies Dan had told her. As newlyweds they were not spending time together, their communication was nonexistent due to the mode and style of their interaction, and they had unrealistic expectations of each other. Their sex life also went south as Nana refused to be intimate with Dan because of her emotional state of mind.

Third Scenario

Donne and Adzo had each separately lived in Toronto as singles and were both born-again Christians. Both being Togolese, they were attracted to each other and dated for a while. They got married after their college/university years. While dating, Donne was very romantic. He would take Adzo out for dinners and movies, send flowers, write poems and do other things that were attractive.

Upon getting married, however, he changed dramatically. He then required Adzo to make his three meals daily, do his and her laundry, keep the house clean (vacuum, mop floors, etc.), satisfy him in the bedroom department, and be the noble woman in Proverbs 31 (this was his favorite line). All the above was required even while they both kept 40-hour-week jobs.

In Donne's mind, he married an African woman who was born in Africa. As such, he expected Adzo to play the traditional role women played in Africa, not keeping in focus that Adzo had been out of Africa for at least 5 years and during that time had seen a lot of the Western values – especially men helping around the house.

Fourth Scenario

Dr. and Mrs. Mensah came to America in 1970. Kofi and Mercy came to pursue higher education with the hope of going back to Ghana after their education was completed. Kofi became a physician, specializing in pediatrics NICU; Mercy got her master's degree in nursing. They both got good-paying jobs and decided to stay on in the United States because of the standard of living, their children (two girls and a boy), and the bad economy back home.

Their children grew older and became of marrying

age. This created a major problem in this very connected but inflexible family. All three kids were born and raised in America (they only visited Ghana twice in their whole lives). The aggressive Mrs. Mensah wanted her kids to marry educated Ghanaians just like them. While Dr. Mensah would have liked them to do this as well, he did not force the issue. To him, the kids' happiness with whomever they married was important as well. The differences of opinion created conflicts in the Mensah household.

Kofi Jr., the first child and only boy of the Mensah family, met a Nigerian girl (Kofo) at work; both were Africans by heritage but American in citizenship and culture (they were both first-generation Americans). Mrs. Mensah reluctantly accepted Kofo (because she was a Christian and an African – she would prefer that to an American) but insisted on conducting a family background check of Kofo's family here in America.

Kofi Jr. and Kofo are now married and as far as they

are concerned they might as well be African-Americans, because that's the culture they've known all their lives.

Mrs. Mercy Mensah is still not giving up on her girls marrying Ghanaians.

Fifth Scenario

Pete and Maryam are Ethiopians who were introduced to each other at NYU (New York University) at a program during Black History Month. Pete graduated, went on to get his MBA and worked for a prestigious accounting firm; Maryam got her degree in political science. Pete and Maryam agreed she should stay home for some years while they raise their children, but that she would eventually go to law school.

Pete is from a middle-class family in Ethiopia; his family in Africa needs support from him to live above the poverty line. Maryam, however, is the daughter of a high-ranking officer attached to the United Nations from Ethiopia. Pete resented the intrusion of his in-laws from the beginning, especially when baby Makeba arrived and his mother-in-law moved in with them for a whole month without his final approval.

Pete also has a new dilemma: His extended family in Ethiopia lives in a run-down house and has been pressuring him to do something about their standard of living by renovating the existing house or building a new one.

CHAPTER FIVE

Conflict Resolution – African, Western, or Biblical?

The difference in religious beliefs, culture, language, and moral values does affect how we resolve conflicts from one continent to another. While the Yoruba people in Nigeria would invite family elders to resolve marital disputes, the Zulus would go to a mediator who would perform rites to appease the people and their gods. John and Mary Smith in Omaha, Neb., would seek help from a marriage therapist.

As Christians (regardless of cultural background), the Bible should form the basis of our culture when in doubt of what to do. In Matthew 18, Jesus gave us the principle of resolving conflict. If people offend you, go to them and tell them what they have done. If they apologize, then the conflict is over. If not, take a witness with you and talk with them again. If they apologize, then the conflict is over. If they still refuse to apologize, then take the case to the church leadership and their judgment should be final on the case.

In applying this principle to marital disputes, couples are encouraged to communicate. Learn as much on communication between husband and wife as possible to help in this.

If the couple cannot solve the dispute, then they should seek external assistance. A lay marriage counselor would be a good start; he or she can then suggest a marriage therapist, psychologist or psychiatrist. If this counsel is not received by the counselee then the church leadership, senior pastor or board of elders can make the final judgment on the conflict.

Resolving conflict does not mean we have a winner or a loser. Rather, it means we've come to an agreement on what to do – even if it is adopting one of the ideas on the table.

There are some basic steps in conflict resolution that are universal:

1. Setting a time to talk to each other without distractions.

2. Identifying the conflict issue, and separating this issue from the person.

3. Identifying each other's role in creating the conflict and acknowledging it.

4. Identifying possible solutions to the conflict.

5. Adopting one solution and working hard at doing it.

6. Meeting regularly (weekly) to talk about each other.

While going through the basic steps to resolve conflict:

- Avoid using words like "Never" and "Always".

- Make no reference to each other's family during the conflict.

- Keep the conflict between the two of you; don't get the kids involved.

- Don't refer to past conflicts.

- Always start talking to each other with endearing words.

When Jesus was asked what the greatest of the commandments is, he said, "Love the Lord thy God with all thine heart and with all thine soul, and love your neighbor as yourself." When we love someone we choose to do extraordinary things for them; because Christ loved us, he died on the cross. Let us seek to put others ahead of ourselves (especially our spouses) when making decisions.

Resolving Peculiar African Marriage Conflicts

Marriage itself brings conflicts, because it's a union of two individuals with different personalities and families of origin who each want to do things their own way. There are conflicts that are universal to any marriage, like communication, infidelity and sex, raising children, stress, anger and a host of others.

However, when we bring two cultures together, that in itself creates a new dynamic of issues.

The following are conflicts peculiar to African couples (couples who grew up in Africa and have the culture within them and are now married) living in a Western-cultured country.

Public Displays of Affection

A visit to a park, shopping mall, cinema, or beach during summer in any city in America or Europe at any time of the day or day of the week would show couples holding hands or lying on a blanket together, or doing things with each other that show affection (there is no age limit to those who do this). There is no shame in publicly showing affection with one's spouse.

In a culture where the man has more than one wife, showing undue public affection to any one of them might bring jealousy and a major "fight" within the household.

With Western education becoming predominant both in Africa and with Africans traveling to Europe and America for it, the practice of marrying many wives is changing to marrying only one. The affectionate displays of love seen in Western countries, however, are still not practiced. Growing up, I doubt if my Dad saw public displays of affection between his parents. I did not see him show any public affection to my Mom (he would tell jokes and make her laugh, but would not touch her in public). I remember Ola trying to hold my hand in public during my first few months after arriving in the United States in 1993. It was very odd and I could not return the favor, especially in church. Years later I counseled a Nigerian couple who had the same uncomfortable issue. While the woman wanted to touch her husband in public, he wanted no part of it except in the privacy of their house (they had lived in the U.S. for 25 years at the time I counseled with them).

The public display of love is something natural to

women because they are emotional, and the public show of affection is important since it indicates ownership and territory demarcation. A woman sees issues from an emotional standpoint and the display of these emotions also comes naturally.

In Africa the physical display of affection in public is frowned on. Couples showing such behavior are usually called names or sometimes extended family might insinuate that the husband must have taken a love potion to publicly display affection to his wife. Women who show romantic love to their husbands in public are usually nicknamed "Ruth – *Aboko ku*" in Western Nigeria (Ruth, the wife who will die for her husband).

Upon arriving in a Western culture a woman quickly adapts to the public display of affection because of her very nature, but the man takes a while longer because he has to figure it out in his head and it is not a natural tendency for him.

These African men often express the opinion that

holding hands in public does not mean love and it is a Western culture that may or may not be adapted. My typical answer during counseling is that the public display of affection is not Western, it is Biblical. King Solomon showed public affection to his wife the Shulammite woman in the book Song of Songs. Showing affection to your wife in public gives her a sense of security (wards off other women) and pride. In Chapter 2 of the Song of Songs, verse 4, the Shulammite woman said, "He has taken me to the banquet hall, and his banner over me is love," meaning King Solomon has declared her as his territory to the entire kingdom and the flag he flies over this new territory is **love** (flying a flag over a territory means ownership).

Romance

Romance is another area of culture shock. In early 1993, I was a car salesman (for 5 months) and I can tell you that Saturday is the busiest day in car sales. Upon returning home after a 12-hour Saturday, I found that Ola had prepared a Japanese meal with candlelight – the main light was turned off and we were supposed to sit on the floor to eat. When I opened the door and turned the light on I could not understand why I would be eating such a meal after a 12-hour workday. Needless to say, I killed the romantic mood by making myself an African meal (Eba – Yoruba meal) at that time of the night.

In counseling with many African men, I find romance to us is sex and nothing more, but now we have to deal with sending cards and flowers, doing spontaneous loving acts (like occasionally getting away with the wife), and the romantic prelude before sex which we never saw growing up.

Being romantic to each other is actually not a cultural thing, but Biblical as well. Just because we never saw our parents do it in Africa does not make it bad. In Ephesians 5, men are told to nurture and cherish their wives; the way to nurture and cherish is by being romantic. Let me encourage my fellow African men: I've spent 10 years (at the time of this writing) in a Western culture and I'm gradually adjusting to holding my wife at picnics or other public settings, I'm sending flowers and cards, and we're doing the occasional getaway (which I happen to like a lot myself).

Communication

This is a major part of any marriage and as Africans we did not see enough – if any – examples of how to communicate in marriage. I remember my Dad's line when he was going out, "I'm going out." Mom's question was always, "To where? Work? Friend's house?" I bet my Dad grew up with his father doing the same. Men in rural Africa congregate at night to drink palm-wine and talk, while those in the city belong to clubs that usually take them away from home and spending time with their spouse and family. Communication is therefore left to when the wife asks for money or when social occasions are being planned within the immediate family or the extended family.

It is common to hear a couple in Europe or America say they have weekly dates so they can invest in their marriage and talk. They also may have family nights. While nothing holds back a couple in Africa from doing the same, it is not culturally accepted so couples shy away from doing it. (It is difficult to do it once they leave their country of origin also.)

Growing up in Lagos, Nigeria, for 26 years I never knew a family where the parents had dated alone or had family nights. In my 10 years of staying in American cities, however, I have noticed couple date nights are not only common but churches even organize them.

Learning how to communicate – even if it's not on a "date night" – would ease a lot of tension. Couples should:

1. Realize that conflicts (in whatever form) are natural and are supposed to make the marriage strong.

2. Realize that unresolved conflicts don't go away but are buried, only to resurface later.

3. Realize that their spouse is a friend and not an enemy (even if it doesn't seem like it).

4. Realize that communication reduces fear and anger and encourages trust in the relationship.

5. Realize that communicating might require changes in their own viewpoint on an issue, as long as it's what is best for the relationship.

6. Realize that communication reduces stress in marriage and uncontaminated information is obtained.

When communicating:

1. Couples need to pay full **attention** to each other, listening not only with their ears but with mind and body as well. Respond with non-verbal gestures, maintain eye contact, and listen for speech tone and inflections.

2. Couples need to **acknowledge** what their spouse is saying by gently nodding their head or responding with comments such as, "That sounds important" or "I can see that you're really concerned."

3. Couples need to say or do things that **invite** the spouse to keep talking about the issues. Don't respond in anger when tough issues are brought up. When talking, use inviting sentences such as, "Tell me more" or "Is there anything more you

want me to know?"

4. Couples need to **summarize** what they've heard their spouse say to ensure understanding before they respond. To summarize, you repeat in your own words what you've heard and ask your spouse to confirm.

5. Couples need to **ask** open-ended questions that would fill in any missing information after they've discussed an issue. "Do you have any other suggestions regarding what we have said?"

Kunle and Lonpe, Dan and Nana, Donne and Adzo, and the Mensahs would have reduced a lot of their stress if they had realized that their conflicts would not disappear and that – rather than avoiding each other – talking about the conflicts would help. They need to set up time for themselves on a regular basis to communicate and invest in each other. Talking about issues does not necessarily mean agreeing to the other's viewpoint. It means two God-fearing people are trying to find a common ground on whatever issue is at hand. It also helps to remember that sometimes agreeing to disagree is a solution.

Past and Present Life

Many Africans dream of immigrating to a developed country for several reasons. Some want to get the Western education, which puts you in a different social class when you return home; some want to escape the poverty brought on by the economy of most African states; and others want to escape war brought on by ethnic rivalry or religion.

Whatever the reason for leaving Africa, once you get to your host country you have to begin life again. Perhaps this means starting from the very low-end jobs that have a high turnover, such as working at fast-food chains, driving cabs, being a car salesperson or many more like that. The key, however, is not to lose sight of why you emigrated: "To take advantage of the market economy and political freedom, providing a better standard of living for your family and yourself." It helps to remember that your dream is achievable in a developed and free society, but it will not be provided on a platter of gold; in most cases you will have to work twice as hard as the citizens of your host country.

I know a physician who came to America and worked in a fast-food restaurant for years before passing his exams. Today he is an expert in his specialty in the state of Texas. I am also aware of a dentist who immigrated to London and for years worked as a dental assistant even though she passed the required certification exams that qualified her to practice in England. She went back to school (despite spending years in her country of origin's dental school, whose certification is recognized in England). Today she is a successful dentist in a city outside London. My wife, Ola, also started from the bottom. When she came back to America at age 21, she worked as a nursing assistant full time while going through a county college. She later transferred to a four-year college and then went to medical school for her M.D. and M.P.H. degrees. Somewhere in those years she got married and had two kids (she is my **hero**).

A lot of Africans dwell on who they used to be (professors, bank managers, etc.), thereby creating undue stress and an erosion of pride that adversely affect their families and themselves. The key is to forget who you used to be in your country of origin, and concentrate on becoming who you want to be in your country of residence.

Methods of Conflict Resolution

As Africans we are told on our wedding day that the union is between both families and really not between the bride and groom alone. Extended family plays a major role in resolving disputes. This extended family is missing once an emigrant is out of Africa. While some do not miss it, some do miss their parents' or grandparents' advice.

For couples who have relied on their extended family as a support mechanism before leaving Africa, it becomes very critical to seek outside help for disputes that they cannot solve together. My recommendations would be:

1. Settle in a community full of your country's people such as New York City, London, Houston, etc.

2. Seek out elders within the community who share your faith and principles of Christ. I would even suggest you adopt older, God-fearing African couples as mentors. We have been blessed to

mentor many couples (Africans and Caribbeans included).

3. Seek out Evangelical or Pentecostal churches with African roots or, if possible, churches with a pastor from your country. Such a pastor might understand the cultural aspects of your conflict when dealing with both of you.

The first step to always resolving disputes is to talk it out between each other in love and with humility of the mind. If this does not work, seek help from the elders in your community or church. If professionals are needed, do not be afraid to go to a Christian psychologist or a marriage therapist.

Spiritual Beliefs

Theologians call the form of African religion "Animism" – this form of religion sees the physical world as interpenetrated by spiritual forces, both personal and impersonal to the extent that objects carry spiritual significance and events have spiritual causes. While we have accepted Christ and have confessed Him, the animistic beliefs permeate our thinking. A Nigerian senior pastor once told me, "When you leave Nigeria, the demons transfer your file to whatever country you are going." As a widely traveled Christian speaker and congregant, I have observed that when speaking to predominantly African congregations topics that deal with "spiritual warfare" generate a more "emotional" response than doing a practical doctrinal teaching.

An African couple I know had serious conflicts, including communication problems, anger issues, pride, lack of respect and physical abuse. I was contacted to assist, and after reviewing the problems I suggested both parties should remain apart while they each saw a Christian marriage therapist in their state.

The counselor would determine when the couple should move back in together based on the progress during their sessions. The elders from the community-based church overrode my recommendation; they told the guy to do some stuff (like paying some amount) to show his attitude change and an increased dosage of fasting and prayer was recommended. Unfortunately, after prayer and fasting for several days the issues that caused the conflicts were never dealt with (his anger, her communication style, etc.). She moved back home only for the physical abuse to occur again.

While spiritual warfare is real, and the Bible tells us so, it also tells us how to overcome by using our weapons of warfare – belt of truth, breastplate of righteousness, gospel of peace, shield of faith, helmet of salvation, sword of the Spirit and continual prayer (*Ephesians 6:10-18*). Our part in spiritual warfare is obedience.

Because of our spiritual beliefs, we Africans

always blame the devil, someone else or circumstances for our wrong. We hardly ever admit what we did wrong outright. This attitude affects the marital relationship. The emphasis is solely on prayer and fasting to attack the demon. While that is true and very real, counseling from qualified people to seek Biblical insight is also very important. Prayer will absolutely help an alcoholic or an angry person but going through a detoxifying program or anger management class would help as well.

Selecting a Spouse

As the children of African immigrants grow older in Western countries and are ready for marriage, they are attracted to peers who are not necessarily of the same color or from the same country, same culture or even same continent. (The daughter of an African president recently married a white minister in Europe in July 2002).

These dynamics are creating major conflicts between parents on one hand and their children on the other hand. Some parents are adamant about their kids marrying from the same country (or even the same tribe within their country of origin). Some parents even encourage their kids to travel back to their country of origin to pick a spouse.

While I acknowledge the problem that marrying from a different culture can bring, the basis and foundation of selecting a spouse should be that he or she has a personal relationship with Christ, which usually comes with exhibiting fruits of the spirit – peace, joy, love, kindness, meekness, patience, goodness, faithfulness, and self-control.

A marriage whose cornerstone is Christ will face its share of problems but with the willingness to humble themselves and be obedient to the word of God, victory is guaranteed in the marriage (even when the wind blows and hail comes).

Choosing a spouse from their current base or traveling back to Africa to pick a spouse both have advantages and disadvantages. What is important, however, is that both parties have a committed relationship with Jesus Christ.

My recipe for choosing a life partner is found in Genesis 24, when Abraham's servant went on a journey to choose a partner for Isaac. Usually two people are attracted to each other because of physical attributes, intellect, financial clout or personality. The reason for marriage, however, should be:

1. Personal relationship with God, verse 3 (marrying a Canaanite would mean serving a foreign god other than Jehovah).

2. Person of faith, verses 57-58 (without seeing Isaac, Rebekah agreed to go with Eliezer).

3. Godly character, verses 15-25 (because of her character, she offered to help a stranger by drawing water from the well).

4. Reputation in the community, and among friends and family members, verses 55 and 60 (her family was very sorry to see her go, because she was well liked).

5. Obedience to authority. (Rebekah was a daughter who honored her parents.)

6. Revealed by God, verse 7. (Abraham told Eliezer that Jehovah would send His angel ahead of him. Eliezer himself prayed that God would reveal the woman to him as well.)

7. Have a servant's heart, verses 15-25. (Rebekah fetched a minimum of 300 gallons of water

from a well – not from a tap – and she willingly did it.)

Joint Account Based on Trust

Having a joint account in Africa is almost impossible, as the culture frowns against such things. Men always have been seen as the sole provider; their incomes are never disclosed to their spouses because they have too many wives. This culture was passed from generation to generation.

Subsequent generations adopted this unfortunate culture because of greed, lack of trust and adultery. As long as a husband provides minimally for the house, he is hailed as a good husband. A good wife is a woman who accepts the wrongs of the husband as long as he provides enough for her to get jewelry, get house-helps, buy expensive clothing, etc.

Upon getting to a capitalist Western culture, this ideology becomes impossible because both husband

and wife go to work and government taxes take a chunk of the income. Combining income ends up being the best way to deal with the bills that come in droves. In counseling with Africans, I have seen many forms of joint accounting (other than a total joint account) devised just to avoid putting money together. None has worked. Having a joint account breeds trust between the husband and wife, enhances communication, and provides the family with a unified budget against the standard of living in a Western culture.

Dealing with In-Laws

The way extended family gets involved in a nuclear family situation in Africa can be overwhelming. Sons take the opinions of their Mothers over that of their wives on situations affecting his family, and daughters delight in what their parents say more than what their husbands say.

A relationship that does not have unity in Africa

before going over to Europe or America will still have in-laws problems.

I have a friend whose wife is not well liked in his family. He came to America and lived alone for about 3 years. In this period he was able to send large sums of money to his extended family anytime he liked. His immediate family (wife and two kids) soon received their visas and joined him in the United States.

The frequency and amount of money he sent home to his extended family quickly reduced and the extended family blamed the woman for the reduced money and frequency. The wife, on the other hand, did not even know how much the husband earned, but bills and the expenses of having the family around weighed on my friend.

Dealing with in-laws from a foreign country could be a blessing in disguise and we ought to take advantage of it.

1. The husband and wife should always communicate about each other's family. Each spouse needs to let his or her extended family know in clear terms that "Whatever you tell me, I'll share with my spouse" and that decisions are made together. A couple once told me about a mother who called the daughter in-law when they were leaving Africa and said to her, "A woman does not share all her money with her husband." Unknown to the wife, the mother-in-law had shared the same statement with her own son. Years later they were relaxing at home (they had started a joint account when they moved to America) and were talking about the mother-in-law when they both realized she said the same thing to both of them.

2. When issues arise with extended family, each person should take on their own family. The

husband should take on his family and the wife her family. If your families in Africa expect more financial help from you and your family, don't have the wife call his family or have the husband call her family. Each person should pick up the phone and tell the family why they won't be getting more than what is already being sent home.

3. There must be mutual respect for each other's family members. The Bible commands us to respect our elders so we might live long on earth. Our spouse's parents are elders to us and should be accorded due respect. Getting respect from each other's family depends on how you present each other to your respective families. If you present your husband as cranky, he can expect cranky treatment from them. If you present your wife as a lazy, good-for-nothing wife, you can be

sure she'll be treated as such.

4. Allocate a certain amount to send monthly to both your family and your spouse's family. (Remember: God is their source. You are only supplementing, and no amount would be sufficient anyway.) When there are emergency expenses like school fees, marriage, etc., they are treated separately, but in agreement.

5. Families in Africa have different views of living in Europe or America. They imagine your lifestyle based on pictures you send home. They may make demands such as, "I'm dying, I need money right away" or "You need to come and build a house so we can have a decent living here," not realizing that you have many bills too and providing for your own family does not come cheap. While it is very OK to take care of

extended family, it should be within your immediate family budget and agreed upon between the husband and the wife.

6. When talking with your extended family back home, refrain from discussing the conflicts you had with your husband or wife. Instead, discuss those conflicts with a local counselor or your church pastor. Your extended family will not come to London or Chicago (or wherever you are) to help resolve the problem. Instead, they will hold on to the awful story you told them about your wife or husband for years and react to your story even after you both have forgotten the particular incident. When you call (phone) home to Africa, tell them how everyone is doing and about the kids, your jobs, the weather, etc. Except for life-threatening illness, keep the bad news to yourself. You can still tell them to pray

for you in a general way (health-wise, financial, etc.) without airing all your problems.

7. When in-laws visit from Africa, men especially should continue to do the household chores they were doing before their Mom's visit. From interviews I have conducted, I have had two women tell me their husbands' attitudes changed when their mothers were visiting; they did not want to do anything in the house except to come home and ask for their food.

At a recent barbecue to honor some visiting friends from Africa, I was in charge of the grill. As the guests started to arrive, a young man came up to me and said, "This is why I don't like America – a big man like you is cooking! In Nigeria, *Me-Suya* would be doing this." I laughed and dismissed his comment. As the next set of guests arrived, one of them took my picture and said he wanted to show it to his friends in Africa, that it is OK for a man to be in charge of cooking.

(*Me-Suya* – a hired help who does barbecue at parties)

CHAPTER SIX

Enjoying Canaan

Whenever we are operating in God's geographical will He blesses us. In Genesis 12:1-3 God told Abram, "Leave your country, your people and your father's household and go to the land I will show you. (1) I will make you into a great nation, and (2) I will bless you; (3) I will make your name great, (4) and you will be a blessing. (5) I will bless those who bless you, (6) and whoever curses you I will curse; (7) and all peoples on earth will be blessed through you."

The above promise was made to Abram by God

when He instructed Abram to move to a land that He would show him. However, this same promise is also being fulfilled by Africans living in Western countries. Examples include: Pastor Matthew Ashimolowo in London, Kofi Annan and Adebayo Ogunlesi in New York, the many mayors in America of African descent, and African sports celebrities such as Hakeem Olajuwon, Dikembe Mutombo, etc. We live in a small city (about 600,000 people) in Midwestern America and we know at least 20 African physicians (in varying specialties, from family practice to surgery).

All of these Africans have a story to tell about how their journeys began. Some came as students and paid their way through college while working 40-hour weeks and raising children at the same time. Some came as professionals but had to do menial jobs before passing the various certification exams.

One common thing is how every one of them kept the vision in focus of why they left their country of origin and therefore today are respectable citizens in their country of residence. Western countries – because of their capitalist structure – offer a smart and hard-working person the opportunity to be rich and live a comfortable lifestyle.

The Israelites sojourned in Egypt and came out with riches. Many Europeans came to America after the Second World War and are now multimillionaires with families that are closely knitted.

The secrets to achieving your vision and sustaining your marriage in a foreign land are:

1. Realizing that your God is still God, irrespective of your geographical location. Study his words (Bible) and seek his face (prayer) day and night for direction. Deuteronomy 28:1-6 says, "If you fully obey the Lord your God and carefully follow all his commands I give you today, the Lord your God will set you high above all the

nations on earth. All these blessings will come upon you and accompany you if you obey the Lord your God: You will be blessed in the city and blessed in the country. The fruit of your womb will be blessed, and the crops of your land and the young of your livestock – the calves of your herds and the lambs of your flocks. Your basket and your kneading trough will be blessed. You will be blessed when you come in and blessed when you go out." God blesses obedience to his word, not your geographical location or the economy of where you live.

2. Having realistic expectations. Changing geographical location from a poor country to a rich country does not solve all problems. Rich countries have problems that they deal with as well; there are people in Europe and America living below poverty lines and they depend on

government subsidies for daily existence. Lack of communication in your marriage in Africa is still going to be there in America. Most Western nations require certain work hours with fixed income. When this income is not sustaining the household people pick up a second job, thereby taking time away from their families. There is also the stress of commute in Western countries. While many studies have been done on how to communicate, many families in Western cultures find it difficult to achieve because of their lifestyle. As immigrants, be ready to work through any conflict that arises in your relationship and seek professional help when needed for your marriage.

3. Having a vision of what you want to achieve and giving yourself a flexible timeline to achieve those things. God had revealed to Joseph that he was going to be a great person

someday. Joseph, however, went through tough times before becoming a prime minister in a foreign land. He was a slave at Potipher's house, where he became the chief servant because of his administrative skills. While in prison he also became a leader. These administrative skills served him well as the prime minister in Egypt. Dream interpretation was God's supernatural intervention in Joseph's life. Like Joseph, we all have a gift or talent that we need to put into practice in the land where we are sojourning. We then need to allow God to supernaturally work through us using the gift he has deposited in our lives. Whether you are in ministry, the corporate world, government work, car sales, etc., be the best at what you do and have a vision for your family.

4. Keeping the past, present, and future in perspective. Apostle Paul was a Pharisee and a success-

ful attorney who prosecuted Christians. After he had an encounter with Christ on his way to Damascus, he never referred to the person he used to be, but only to the commission that God gave to him to reach the Gentiles with the gospel. Dwelling on who they were in Africa (bank manager, corporate executive, professor, etc.) and their temporary state in their host country (cleaner, fast-food restaurant worker, cab driver, etc.) has dealt severe blows to many men, especially in the area of self-esteem. They usually take out their anger and frustration on their wife and children at home. Let your focus be on what you hope to achieve in your new country of residence.

5. Studying the socioeconomic state of your host country to determine what is needed in the economy both short term and long term. Health

professions (physicians and nurses) are a long-term investment in America and they'll be in demand for some time to come. Determine the best location suitable for your family, whether it is a city with communities from your host country or a suburb that gives you privacy. A lot of Nigerians are crowding the city of London, thinking that is the best place to get jobs; however, many are now moving out and saying to themselves, "Why didn't we do this sooner?" Do not be afraid to change careers; go into nursing, computer programming or networking, medicine, etc. Getting higher degrees puts you in line for promotion in your company or for a better-paying job elsewhere.

6. Studying your host country's attitude to immigrants in your industry. For instance, I have heard from many physicians in England that for

an immigrant physician to become a consultant is like a camel going through the eye of a needle. In the United States, once you achieve the educational requirements, getting to the top of your field or profession is within reach. Corporations reward production, not color or accent; they are driven by the financial bottom line.

7. Making your marriage a priority. As you set out to achieve your financial goals, your marriage should not pay for your corporate achievements. Set time aside for you and your spouse, and then the children. The definition of wealth is not how much you're worth or what is in your bank account. Wealth is what becomes of your children, what your spouse says about you, and what people read on your tombstone when you are gone. Apostle Paul in his letter to Timothy wrote that an overseer must be a man of but one wife,

self-controlled, respectable, able to teach, gentle, not a lover of money, and must manage his family well with his kids obeying him. A study of millionaires in America shows 85 percent of them are married (and use pickup trucks) and they attribute their success to their spouses.

8. Getting rid of African myths that are not based on the Bible. Growing up in Africa many of us heard stories of how "Only a weak husband helps around the house or discloses his income to his wife" or "Wives should not share everything with their husbands," etc.

Twice the Bible reminds us that two shall become one, meaning once we marry God sees the husband and wife as one individual. As such, everything in our lives should become one – our finances, communication with families, goals and visions, raising of godly children, and everything else not mentioned. We need to examine why we are still separating our resources when God sees us as one. Is it trust or lack of it, poor communication, pride, adultery, etc.? If we have any belief that has been etched into us from birth or from our family of origin that hinders intimacy in our marriage, we need to ask God to remove this obstacle so that we can experience the blessing of oneness with our spouse.

References

Ethnicity and Family Therapy, Monica McGoldrick *et. al.*, Guilford Press, 1996

The NIV Study Bible, Zondervan Publishers, 1979

Talking and Listening, Sharon Miller *et. al.*

The Book of Romance, Tommy Nelson, Thomas Nelson Publishers, 1998

Wilderness: A Western Concept Alien to Arctic Cultures, David Klein, arcticcircle.uconn.edu (online article)

To contact

CHRISTIAN COUPLES FELLOWSHIP
INTERNATIONAL, INC.

For a

FAMILY WEEK

BUILDING HEALTHY MARRIAGES SEMINAR

MARRIAGE CONFERENCE

SINGLES CONFERENCE

Also if you are interested in starting a CCFI Chapter

Christian Couples Fellowship International, Inc.,
6711 North 102 Avenue
Omaha NE 68122
402-933-0268
christiancouples@att.net

Or visit our website
WWW.CHRISTIANCOUPLESFELLOWSHIP.COM

CPSIA information can be obtained at www.ICGtesting.com
Printed in the USA
LVOW11s0055170415

434915LV00001B/45/P

9 781591 604488